Knowledge

Vs.

Wisdom

Knowledge

Over the centuries it is a proven fact that mankind is endowed with knowledge to survive and develop. The instinct to hunt, build, increase, and develop society's progression.

Knowledge of many types of things is bestowed on each person. In some cases, special knowledge about certain things like math and science has enhanced civilization.

Many times, knowledge is gained simply by sight or hearing. The ability to build or lead often comes from the capability of having knowledge gained by insight.

Knowledge is the state of knowing and the perception of facts and truths. Many men and women are credited with this perception that has improved society.

Wisdom

Many of us have knowledge and can do many things in life. We maintain ourselves and our families because of the knowledge that we have.

However, the ability to be wise means that we can take knowledge of what is true or right and make judgment to actions with special insight.

A wise act comes from having knowledge and the insight of wisdom to carry it through with truth and justice. Therefore, knowledge without wisdom can be fruitless and even dangerous in the wrong hands.

Contents

Grow Knowledge into Wisdom

It is easy to grow knowledge just get started increase you base with the following steps:

- Listen to what is happening around you instead of talking.
- Read newspapers and informational books.
- Inquire about others regarding current events.
- Be part of your neighborhood events.

- Eat healthy foods that improve your cognitive thinking.
- Exercise helps your body and your mind.

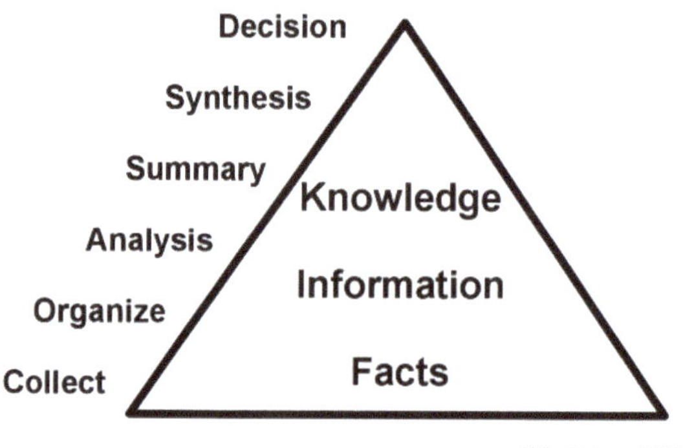

Knowledge Base to increase Wisdom

While we may assume that everyone has a certain amount of knowledge about life, it does vary from individual to individual. The knowledge base does not always apply to every person. Do you use the six steps to increase your knowledge base and make informative decisions showing you have wisdom?

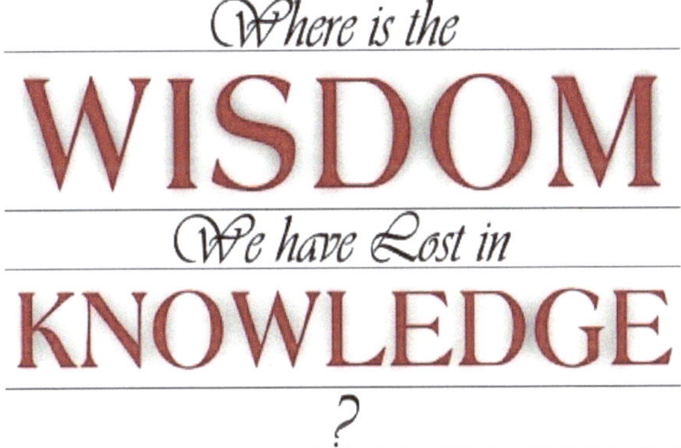

When using knowledge without wisdom, it can be lost. It is fruitless to have a head full of knowledge but not the wisdom to use it. That is proven over the centuries by the rich and the poor. Great leaders have fallen and nations with them because their head was full of knowledge but lacked the wisdom to use it. Therefore, men have followed these leaders to destruction. It is not always advisable to follow someone without applying your own wisdom. Be not deceived through the powerful rhetoric of these men. Instead, use your ability to think rational in order, to gain wisdom from any situation at hand.

Many times, we have lost our ability to gain wisdom by the overabundance of knowledge that is not approved by wisdom. Our leaders and states people may provide us with many comforts because of their authority.

But when authority is not enough, and knowledge is needed then all is lost without wisdom to use the knowledge at hand. It takes the knowledge of many to help the much-needed wisdom of one.

Knowledge without Wisdom in the Garden

When God created Adam then Eve, he told them not to eat of the tree of forbidden fruit. This was the tree of **Good and Evil**. Translated as the tree that gave them **Knowledge.**

The fact, it did not give them **Wisdom**. The *"Devil"* was cast as the one who enticed Eve into biting the tree to gain both ***Knowledge and Wisdom***. In fact, the act was done with the **Knowledge** that they would learn the difference between **Good and Evil.**

Unfortunately for the couple, they needed the knowledge to use this wisdom and had to learn that. It could not be obtained in the garden and therefore, they were cast out into the world to gain wisdom.

Knowledge without Wisdom - Old World Style

The world did not seize to be but populated and grew. Humans procreated over time, and cities began to grow. The invention of the wheel and fire helped civilization. It was the wisdom used that made these inventions helpful to create society.

While this was the start of civilization, much needed to be done to advance man. Many have proclaimed that mankind was able to advance because of interference by aliens. That aliens come to earth and endowed men with knowledge to build and grow.

Others claim it is over time that man's wisdom helped him along. In other words, knowledge grew with wisdom and so did civilization.

In that day, villages started up and cities became larger. Some men ventured into other parts of the world. Those explorers are credited with creating different societies in different parts of the world. The people who stayed behind are credited with growing society to its modern state.

Many different societies grew in those days such as:

- Romans
- Greeks
- Egyptians

- Israelites
- Aztecs
- Mayans
- Chinese
- Europeans

It is not to say that there were not many others also, as this world grew in leaps and bounds.

Knowledge that was shared became wisdom to others that enabled us the way of life we now enjoy. It is often said that not one man created life that could exist in this world, but it was the "One God" who watched us flourish.

The "Old World" was full of many different heroes who fought battles to save civilizations. It was also full of men who had the wisdom to enhance the way of life that we needed for survival.

Knowledge Introduced Wisdom - New World Style

The coming of Christ ushered in real knowledge that gave man the wisdom he needed to progress and succeed in life. The early years were barbaric to say the least. This man known as the son of God was crucified. He gave us a new way of life that showed us how to "Love One Another."

Wisdom is great! Love is greater! That fact needed to be learned by all of us. It was not only needed but it was a must if we are to survive in this world and become a part of the Kingdom of God. Christ came to show us the way, the truth, and the light. Every civilization has guidelines to enable them to be human.

Ancient Roman Modern Civilization

In the days of old Rome, Rome was known to have the most modern of civilizations. It had many men of knowledge but few with wisdom. Instead the men were all self-centered and only wanted possessions.

Still with all this greed and gluten, it seems there were men with wisdom.

The clock and calendar were invented during this time. Water systems and other major inventions that are carried through to this day to our modern society. The Romans had many ideas to a modern world. But they did not know how to love and care. They did not have Jesus in their hearts and minds.

Modern civilizations have risen and fallen because of the lack of wisdom by its leaders. Many of the leaders were cruel without love in their hearts. But because they had many who gave them knowledge on what was happening in their country they could conquer.

They lost their status and even the nation because of the lack of wisdom. It was one thing to be filled with knowledge but without the wisdom to act upon it all was lost.

Knowledge and Wisdom - Greatest Inventions

The fact remains that technology today has brought forth many new inventions that has greatly improved the world today. The world has improved because the invention of tools improved society.

It is impossible to note all the important tools and who invented them, but we will try to name a few along the way that greatly made the world a better place.

Invention #1 Wheel

We were limited on how far we could travel and the amount of content we could carry until the invention of the wheel. The wheel remains in our society and has been improved over centuries moving us along into the future.

Invention #2 Nail

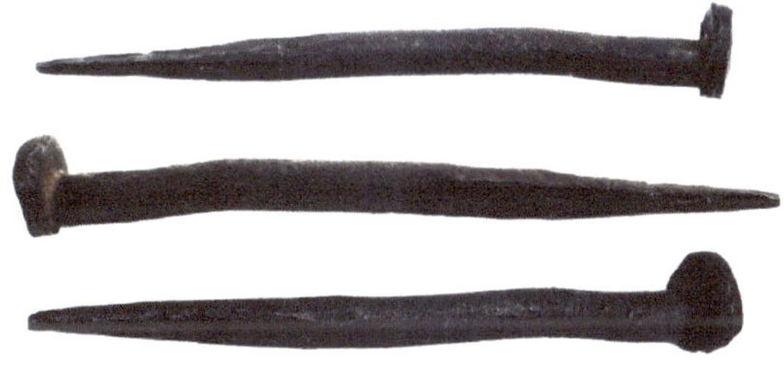

Nails help keep the world from crumbling down. Without nails homes could not be held together. Nails were created over 2,000 years ago in time of the Roman Empire. Nails were a wonderful invention for society, and it helps hold it together.

Invention #3 The Compass

The Mariners traveled by the stars for centuries but that did not always work. Often, they would lose their way. The Chinese invented the compass. It was assumed around the 9th century.

The first compass was made from a lode stone, which is a magnet iron ore. The compass soon passed to the Europeans and the Arabians. It is this reason that people were able to travel and become explorers.

Invention #4 The Printing Press

The German Inventor Johannes Gutenberg made the first printing press. It made it possible to make massive prints of information. The Bible is a perfect example of the importance a printing press. Today, the Internet has become the instrument whereby information is spread worldwide.

Invention #5 Internal Combustion Engine

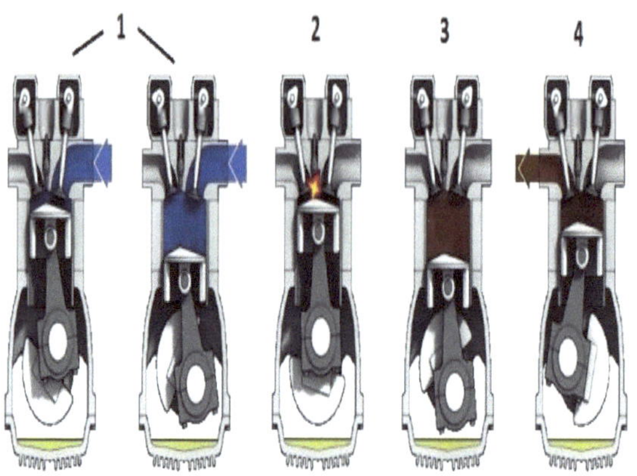

Many scientists worked on these machines over the century and this helped with modern equipment. Today, many things are created and work to improve society because of the internal combustion engine.

Invention #6 Telephone

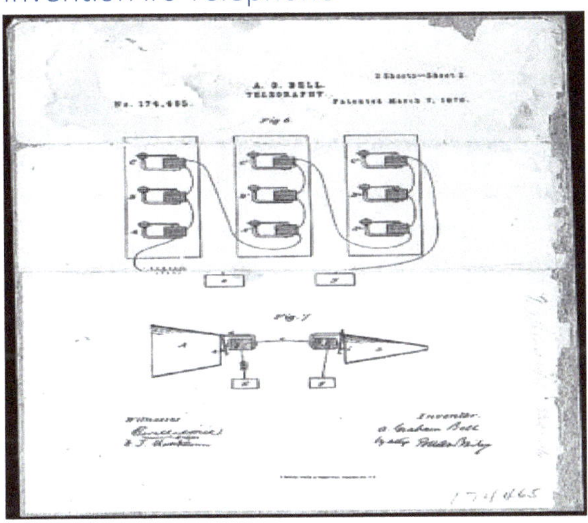

The best form of communication is the telephone. Electronic voice transmission was very important. Today, it has improved with the invention of the cell phone and other inventions like the radio and television.

Invention #7 Light Bulb

Natural light has changed the way people look at things in the world. The invention of the light bulb by Thomas Edison made a whole new life style possible for people. It is nice to be able to walk down lighted streets and have light in the home, which is safer than candles.

Invention #8 Penicillin

The invention of Penicillin made life last longer as it was a great medical invention that helped to save life. Infections and diseases were cured with the use of Penicillin. Modern day miracle to say the least as doctors now had something to fight infections.

Invention #9 The Internet

The Internet has proven to be the greatest invention of the modern era. It is the global connection that puts billions of people together.

The internet has united people across the world with a fantastic communication system. We are now able to be together and share life experiences, train, teach, buy, sell, do about everything that keeps humanity alive.

Invention #10 Every Wonderful Thing

Every wonderful thing that this world must have for our life span has been invented. We can travel to the bottom of the ocean and go to world's unknown.

The medical field and the scientific field has advanced so far beyond belief. The problem my friends is that we are not able to change the *human gene* to where we can rid ourselves of hate, strife, jealousy, envy, and all the things that destroy our lives.

With all our modern technological advances **man still destroys man** and even worse because of our knowledge we now are **destroying earth**. The place where we all live is coming apart because of our behavior. That is a true sign that **Knowledge without Wisdom** is destructive in the wrong hands.

Knowledge vs. Wisdom in the New World

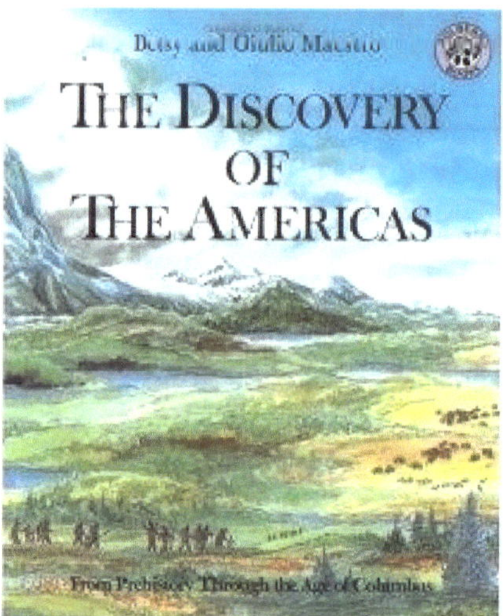

New World

When Columbus discovered America, it gave the Old World the opportunity to change for the better. New land! New people! New life style!

Many things took place over the centuries that were so disappointing and other things that took place help improve the existence of human kind.

The way that the early settlers destroyed the native Indians is a blot on our country. We did not treat them with kindness and love. Instead we showed hatred and distrust. We lost a lot of knowledge from New World people that could have taught us a lot.

We also have the problem of not treating others in the right manner. The idea of slaves carried over from the **"Old World,"** and we did nothing to improve society. Instead, with our little bit of knowledge and no wisdom shown, we heightened the problem.

Our nation would have been divided if it had not been for a great man who had the wisdom to understand the importance of keeping us together.

First, we were a nation of many scattered about the wilderness. There were towns and farms but nothing united. It was time that this great new land had a government and unity.

Few great men like George Washington realized this and were able to unite the people to this end. The wisdom of Washington, Franklin, and others gave us this nation. They helped unite the people and the struggle against the British began. Through war, we were able to drive out the British and soon became one nation under God. The intentions of course were that all men (women) should be free.

Unfortunately, this did not happen because of the great division of man and their thoughts to what it meant to be free. We still had slaves that were not only bought and sold from Africa and the Ivory Coast, but we also had indentured servants from Europe as well.

America was still growing and expanding. People would venture out across the plains into the mountains and on to the southern coast. America finally became settled and one big nation. While people were traveling and starting new cities, they were gaining knowledge.

Many people learn how to survive in this vast wilderness by using the knowledge they had gained from the American Indians and the wisdom to use it.

Knowledge vs. Wisdom in the Industrial Revolution

This is the area in which many inventions come about for the modernization of America. We all know that inventions take place when someone has the wisdom to use their knowledge. Therefore, knowledge is a vital part of society progressing.

We all know that knowledge is something that most all of us possess. It may be limited, or it might be in over abundance, but most "normal" people have knowledge.

The real quest comes with those who possess "wisdom." Not everyone has enough wisdom to achieve great things, be a leader, or even take out the trash. Common sense comes into play for most people, so therefore, they function very well in life. But are not great achievers just the normal average person. Those with great wisdom are able to excel in life and help others to do the same thing. Let's take a look at the things and people who progressed and helped us to be where we are at this moment.

Remember the Industrial Revolution took place between the 18th and 19th century. People left the farms and went to the city

The Industrial Revolution, which took place from the 18th to 19th century, was a period during which predominantly agrarian, rural societies in Europe and America became industrial and urban.

Prior to the Industrial Revolution, which began in Britain in the late 1700s, manufacturing was often done in people's homes, using hand tools or basic machines. Industrialization marked a shift to powered, special-purpose machinery, factories, and mass production.

The iron and textile industries, along with the development of the steam engine played central roles in the Industrial Revolution, which also saw. improved systems of transportation, communication, and banking, which were also major parts of the Industrial movement in that era. While industrialization brought about an increased volume and variety of manufactured goods and an improved standard of living for some, it also resulted in often grim employment and living conditions for the poor and working classes.

Men with great insight became known for their wisdom. The knowledge that was brought forth enhanced life very rapidly around the world. The United States proved to be the leader in world wide industry.

Such men as John Paul Getty, John D. Rockefeller, Thomas Edison, and others made great strides when it came to life improvements. A very important part of our world had exploded. Now knowledge and wisdom were hand in hand together. Many people made great strides in their life. Colleges were at full forces teaching people how to do many good things.

The world was expanding in leaps and bounds then the world was engulfed at war. The war stopped many inventions but also created new inventions by the power of wisdom. War machines, flying machines, new ammunition, and many other different things were created.

Kings of the Hill

The Capitol

United States of America

After World War II, many things took place in the United States of America. Progress was being made in leaps and bounds. However, many of the old stigmas were still around. The various presidents had internal problems that were causing many things to go wrong.

It is true that President Roosevelt had his hands full with winning the war, getting peace treaties in place, and helping nations that had been robbed of their possessions.

Trying to get the world in order again was a major problem. It would take someone with vast knowledge of both America and the outside world. We no longer could be isolationists. We now had to join the world in peace in order to prosper.

President Dwight Eisenhower

On stage for this new time in history was President Dwight David Eisenhower. He brought into the White House his prestige of being a general during the war.

He was one of the true "Kings of the Hill" by being able to help end the war in Korea and also help ease the tensions during the cold war. Truly a remarkable man who showed that he knew how to use his knowledge because he had wisdom beyond his years.

President Ronald Reagan

President Reagan was well known for being a conservative. He was an avid foe of the Soviet Union and helped the

American people when the economy was in terrible condition with his Reaganomics.

He was known as a cherry optimist and a staunch conservative. He was the governor of California and well known as an actor. He made over fifty movies and many times, he was the leading man.

Very charismatic in the movies and in politics. He was endowed with much knowledge and he had the wisdom to use it.

President James Earl Carter Jr.

President Carter was our scientific president. He had peanut farm in Georgia and strived to help the poor. He has been working for a project called Habitat for Humanity to this day providing homes to those who otherwise could not afford a home.

President Richard M. Nixon

President Nixon was the first president to quit the office. The Watergate episode ruined his career, and he full well knew it. He was a man full of knowledge but had very little wisdom when it came to his political affairs. Trusting others led him into trouble and eventually ruined his political career. Due to his involvement in Watergate, President Gerald R. Ford took over office and finished out his term. President Ford was a well-loved man but decided not to run for president.

President John F. Kennedy

One of the most popular presidents of our time was John F. Kennedy. President Kennedy did much to help the poor, unite this country during a time when civil war and crime was being done against the black people. Segregation was stopped. Many things got done to change the ways of America.

Unfortunately, Mr. Kennedy was assassinated and even in this he was able to unite Americans. He was truly a man of knowledge and wisdom. He was a great orator. When he spoke, people listen to him. He began our Medicare program to help those who were on Social Security to have medical care.

He also formulated the program called SSI for those who were not able to draw Social Security. Mr. Kennedy was instrumental in the Civil Rights Movement to help the people of different color to win their rights in society.

The arms race came to ahead when Russia sent missiles to Cuba. The Cuban Crisis could have ended in war, but he was able to prevent that as well and kept foreign powers from coming to this part of the world.

Mr. Kennedy was truly a man with knowledge and the wisdom to use it.

President Barack Obama

President Barack Obama was the 44th President and the first black president that this nation had ever had in office. He worked very hard for the nation and had many great ideas to help change things for the people.

His beautiful wife worked with him in helping the food programs in school, at fast food restaurants etc. He helps bring about health care for those who did not have insurance. It was unfortunate that he had many people in the government who fought against his ideas because of his race. They even walked out one time and went to a motel rather than vote.

While he had many people against him he also had many people who loved him and his family. The nation was a better place because of his tenor in office.

He was born August 4, 1961 in Honolulu, Hawaii. His birth name was Barack Hussein Obama Jr. He was named after his father Barack Hussein Obama who was an economist. His mother was Stanley Ann (Dunham) Obama Soetoro and she was an anthropologist. He married Michelle Robinson Obama on October 3, 1992 and they are still married today. He has two daughters Natasha and Malia. He is a Christian man with strong faith in God.

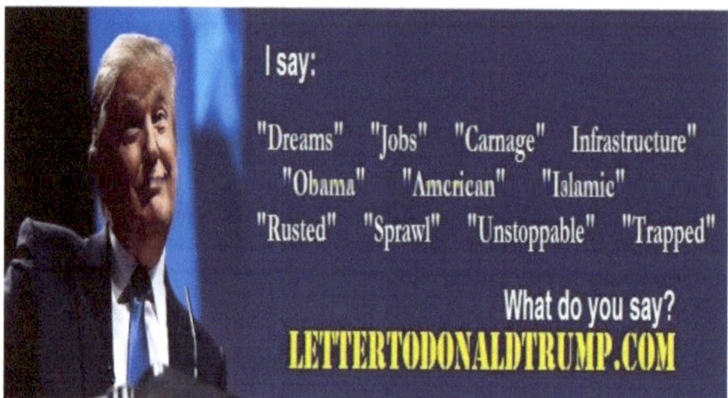

President Donald Trump

President Donald Trump reigns today as our leader. He has proven without a doubt that a man can take knowledge with no wisdom and cause havoc in a nation and the world. America has never been in such turmoil as what this president has created.

We are becoming like the nations in the past that were destroyed internally thanks to his stupidity. He believes that a wall is a solution between nations, that destroying the people who help build this great nation will improve it. He thinks that he is unstoppable. He wants to take us back into the dark ages. We as a nation have been able to go forward until today. The question now is will we survive. The fear is that a foreign power like Russia will finally take over.

Khrushchev had declared that he would bury us during the cold war. The fact is with Donald Trump that might come to pass. We are losing faith with the world of nations and our people are starting to suffer. The point being that Knowledge can be destructive if put into the wrong hands.

 Wisdom is needed to save this great nation and right now we are faced with those who do not have the wisdom to stop the onset of our own destruction Will we parish like Rome? Will we survive and go forth? Only time will tell and show us which path to take.

Knowledge vs Wisdom
For All Human Kind

The fact is no matter who oversees any nation it is the nucleus of the family that counts. In every period many tragedies happen, and many new things are invented. The world goes forward because of the progress. It also seems to come to a halt because of the ignorance that human kind has when it comes to the importance of life. We are blessed because God gave us the ability to procreate and build a family with love. Not because of knowledge or wisdom.

But we hope this book will be a learning tool for each generation.

Knowledge is passed down from generation to generation. It is found that wisdom is something that is obtained by the ability of our people to know how to use the knowledge given to them. It is unfortunate, but wisdom is not an inherit trait.

Be made assured as the world spins around life exists and with the wisdom of some men we will progress and with only knowledge some men will cause destruction. It is the family that counts most of all in every society.

ISBN: 13:978-1985822245

ISBN: 10: 198-5822245